MICROSOFT
WINDOWS 7

With Advanced Features

~~***~~

John Monyjok Maluth

Copyrighted © 2013 **John Monyjok Maluth**

***

Discipleship Press

Website: www.discipleshippress.wordpress.com
Email: maluthabiel@gmail.com
Phone: +254 110 424 822

~~***~~

P.O. Box 28448-00100, Nairobi, Kenya

ISBN: 9781728771571

Library of Congress Control Number: 2022907783

All rights reserved. No part of this book may be reproduced, stored in a retrieval system, or transmitted in any or by any means – electronic, mechanical, photocopying, recording, or otherwise-without prior permission in writing from the copyright holder except as provided by USA copyright law.

HOW TO USE THIS BOOK

This book is for beginners and everyday users who want to feel confident using Windows 7. You do not need a technical background. If you can read, click, and follow simple steps, you can do everything in this guide.

Read it in two ways, depending on your goal.

If you want to learn Windows 7 step by step, start from Part One and continue in order. Do the short practice tasks as you go. That is the fastest way to build real skill.

If you only want to fix a problem or learn one feature, use the table of contents to jump to the chapter you need. Each chapter is written so you can start there without reading the whole book first.

HOW TO PRACTICE WHILE YOU READ

Keep your computer on while reading. Do the steps on your own PC, not only in your head.

After every topic, repeat the action at least two times. Example: if you learn how to create a folder, create two folders, rename them, and delete one. Repetition is how it sticks.

Use a "practice folder" to avoid fear. Create one folder on your Desktop named Practice. Use it for testing. You can delete it later.

If you are worried about making mistakes, remember this. Most actions can be undone. Deleted files can often be restored from the Recycle Bin. Settings can be changed back. This book will point out the few places where you must be careful.

WHAT YOU NEED BEFORE YOU START

A Windows 7 computer, laptop, or desktop.

A mouse (or touchpad) and a working keyboard.

Basic access to your user account. If you are not the administrator, some settings may be locked. The book will tell you when admin permission is required.

Optional but helpful: a USB flash drive for backup and moving files.

HOW INSTRUCTIONS ARE WRITTEN IN THIS BOOK

When you see a path like this:

Start > Control Panel > System and Security

It means: click the Start button, then open Control Panel, then open the section named System and Security.

Click means press the left mouse button once.

Double-click means press the left mouse button two times quickly.

Right-click means press the right mouse button once to open a menu of options.

When you see keyboard keys written like this:

Ctrl + C

Hold Ctrl, then press C once.

Windows 7 on different PCs

Windows 7 may look slightly different on different computers. Some computers use different screen sizes, different brands, and different drivers. Also, Windows 7 has several editions. The main ideas stay the same, even if a button is in a slightly different place or a window looks a little different.

If you cannot find a setting exactly as described, use the search box in the Start menu and type the name of the setting. This is often the fastest route.

KEY TERMS USED IN THE BOOK

Desktop: the main screen you see after you sign in.

Icon: a small picture you click to open a program, file, or folder.

Start menu: the menu that opens when you click the Start button.

Taskbar: the long bar, usually at the bottom of the screen, that shows open programs and shortcuts.

Window: a box on the screen where you work, such as a folder window or a program window.

Dialog box: a smaller window that asks a question or shows options before an action continues.

Control Panel: the main place for changing Windows settings.

File: a single item like a document, photo, music track, or video.

Folder: a container that holds files and other folders.

File extension: the letters after a dot in a file name, like .doc, .jpg, or .mp3. It helps Windows know which program should open the file.

Shortcut: a link to a program or file. A shortcut is not the original item. Deleting a shortcut usually does not delete the real file.

Driver: software that helps Windows communicate with hardware like printers, sound, Wi-Fi, or graphics.

Update: a system improvement that fixes problems and improves security.

Administrator: a user account with full permission to change system settings and install software.

Standard user: a user account with limited permission, used for safer daily work.

KEY LABELS AND ICONS USED IN THIS BOOK

Because this is a practical guide, you will see the same labels repeatedly. They help you know what to do and what to watch for.

[STEP] A direct action you should follow in order.

[TRY IT NOW] A short practice task. Do it on your computer immediately.

[TIP] A faster method, a shortcut, or a helpful habit.

[NOTE] A small detail that prevents confusion.

[WARNING] Something that can cause problems if done wrongly, such as deleting important files or changing critical settings.

[SHORTCUT] A keyboard shortcut or a quick path.

[COMMON PROBLEM] A typical issue beginners face, with a simple fix.

[CHECKLIST] A short list of items you should confirm before you continue.

Safety notes before you begin

Do not download unknown programs to "speed up" your computer. Many are unsafe. Use built-in Windows tools first.

Be careful when changing system settings you do not understand. This book will explain why a setting matters before asking you to change it.

Back up important files before installing Windows, upgrading, or doing major maintenance. If you do not know how yet, read the backup steps first before you proceed.

When you're ready, say "Next…" and I'll write the next section of the book.

CONTENTS

PART ONE: GETTING WINDOWS 7 READY 1

CHAPTER ONE: WHAT WINDOWS 7 IS AND WHAT EDITION YOU HAVE 1

CHAPTER TWO: GETTING A LEGITIMATE COPY AND PREPARING INSTALLATION MEDIA..................................20

CHAPTER THREE: INSTALLING WINDOWS 7 STEP BY STEP 40

CHAPTER FOUR: UPGRADING TO WINDOWS 7 SAFELY ..61

PART TWO: DAILY USE SKILLS (THE FEATURES PEOPLE TOUCH EVERY DAY)...84

CHAPTER FIVE: THE DESKTOP, START MENU, AND TASKBAR 84

CHAPTER SIX: WORKING WITH FILES AND FOLDERS THE RIGHT WAY...108

CHAPTER SEVEN: BUILT-IN HELPERS THAT SAVE TIME .129

BACK MATTER 146

FINAL NOTE TO THE READER 164

PART ONE: GETTING WINDOWS 7 READY

Windows 7 is still one of the easiest Windows versions to learn because the layout is simple, the menus are predictable, and most tasks follow clear steps. Before you install it, upgrade to it, or even start using it seriously, you need to know one thing first.

What exact Windows 7 do you have?

That question matters more than most beginners expect, because the Windows 7 edition and system type decide what features you can use, what upgrades make sense, what drivers you need, and what problems you might face later.

CHAPTER ONE: WHAT WINDOWS 7 IS AND WHAT EDITION YOU HAVE

1) What Windows 7 is (in plain language)

Windows 7 is an operating system. An operating system is the main software that runs your computer. It controls:

- how your desktop looks

- how programs open and close

- how files are stored and found

- how your keyboard, mouse, printer, and Wi-Fi work

- how accounts and passwords work

- how your computer starts up and shuts down

If you think of your computer as a house, Windows 7 is the building plan that decides where the doors are, where the rooms are, and how electricity and water flow. Your programs are the furniture. Your files are the things you own inside.

So when Windows 7 is installed and working well, everything else becomes easier.

2) Why "edition" matters

Windows 7 comes in different editions. An edition is like a "package level." The computer is still Windows 7, but the package changes:

- what tools are included

- what settings you can access

- what network features work

- whether you can join a company domain

- whether advanced security and backup tools are included

Many people only notice this when something does not work, like when they try to join a workplace network, use Remote Desktop, or access advanced backup options.

If you know your edition early, you avoid confusion later.

Windows 7 editions (Starter, Home, Professional, Ultimate)

Here is a beginner-friendly way to understand the editions you will most often see.

Windows 7 Starter

Windows 7 Starter was made for low-power computers, especially small laptops (netbooks) that were popular years ago.

Typical signs you might be using Starter:

- the computer is slower than most
- the screen resolution options are limited
- you have fewer personalization choices
- advanced business features are missing

Starter is fine for basic use: browsing, typing documents, watching videos, and simple office work. But it is not ideal if you want stronger networking features, advanced system tools, or more control.

Windows 7 Home (usually Home Premium)

Many people say "Windows 7 Home" to mean the home edition they bought or received with the computer. On many PCs it is Windows 7 Home Premium.

This edition is made for normal home users. It usually supports:

- daily tasks and normal programs
- personalization features
- home networking features like sharing printers and files
- many common drivers and devices

If your goal is general daily use, Home is often enough.

Windows 7 Professional

Professional is where Windows 7 begins to feel like a work tool rather than only a home tool.

Professional is designed for:

- small businesses

- office work
- advanced networking needs
- users who want more system control

Professional often includes features that Home does not include, such as:

- joining a domain (useful in many workplace setups)
- advanced backup options
- remote access features (depending on setup)
- more control over user accounts and security settings

If you are working in an office, a school environment, or any structured workplace, Professional is commonly the best fit.

Windows 7 Ultimate

Ultimate is the "everything included" edition for regular consumer installation media. It is designed for users who want all available features.

In many cases, Ultimate is used by:

- technicians and advanced users

- people who install Windows themselves often

- people who want every tool available without worrying about limits

Be careful here: Ultimate is not automatically faster than other editions. It mainly includes more features. Speed depends more on your hardware, drivers, and how clean the installation is.

How to check your Windows 7 edition, system type, and version

You should check three things:

1. Your Windows edition

2. Your system type (32-bit or 64-bit)

3. Your version details (Service Pack level and build info)

I will show you several methods. Use the one that feels easiest.

Method A: Check edition and system type using "System" (best for beginners)

This is the simplest method for most people.

Steps

1. Click the Start button.

2. Right-click Computer.

3. Click Properties.

A window will open called "View basic information about your computer."

Look for these lines:

- Windows edition (this tells you Starter, Home, Professional, or Ultimate)

- System type (this tells you 32-bit or 64-bit)

- Installed memory (RAM)

- Processor type

What to write down

- Edition: _____

- System type: _____

- RAM: _____

- Processor: _____

Why this matters

- If you have 32-bit Windows, there are memory limits and some programs will not install.

- If you have 64-bit Windows, your PC can usually use more RAM and run 64-bit programs.

- Knowing the edition helps you follow the right steps later in networking, accounts, and system tools.

Method B: Check version details using "winver" (quick and accurate)

This method tells you the exact Windows version details.

Steps

1. Click Start.

2. In the search box, type: winver

3. Press Enter.

A small window opens showing Windows version information.

Look for:

- "Windows 7"
- the edition line
- the version line
- Service Pack information (if listed)

Why this matters

Some Windows 7 computers have different update levels. If one PC has more updates installed than another, they may behave differently. If you are troubleshooting, this tool helps you confirm what you are really working with.

Method C: Use System Information (msinfo32) for deeper details

This method is helpful if you are preparing for installation, upgrades, drivers, or hardware checks.

Steps

1. Click Start.
2. Type: msinfo32
3. Press Enter.

The System Information window opens.

Key areas to check:

- OS Name (your edition)
- Version (more detail than basic System page)
- System Type (x86-based PC or x64-based PC)
- Installed Physical Memory (RAM)
- BIOS Version/Date

Quick translation

- x86-based usually means 32-bit
- x64-based usually means 64-bit

Method D: Check via Control Panel (useful if Computer is not visible)

If you do not see "Computer" easily, do this:

1. Click Start.
2. Click Control Panel.
3. Click System and Security.
4. Click System.

You will see the same information as Method A.

What "32-bit" and "64-bit" really means

Beginners often ignore this, then later get stuck when a program will not install.

Here is the simple truth:

- 32-bit Windows can run 32-bit programs.

- 64-bit Windows can run most 32-bit programs and also run 64-bit programs.

So 64-bit is usually more flexible.

But your computer must support 64-bit to run 64-bit Windows. Most modern computers do, but many older ones do not.

Why it matters for installing or upgrading

- If your PC is 32-bit, you cannot install 64-bit Windows unless your hardware supports it and you do a clean install.

- Upgrading from 32-bit to 64-bit is not a normal upgrade. It usually requires a clean installation, meaning you must back up everything first.

What you should prepare before installing or upgrading

This section is written to protect you from the two most common beginner disasters:

- losing files
- getting stuck without drivers or internet after installation

Even if you are not installing today, read this. It will save you stress later.

Preparation Step 1: Back up your important files

Before any install or upgrade, back up what matters.

Back up at least these:

- Documents (Word files, PDFs)
- Photos
- Videos
- Music
- Desktop files (many people forget the Desktop)

- Browser bookmarks (if you can export them)

- Any work folders you created

Where to back up

- An external hard drive is best.

- A USB flash drive can work for smaller data.

- Another computer can work if you can copy through a network.

Simple backup habit

Create one folder on the backup drive called:

Backup Before Windows 7 Install

Copy your important folders into it.

Preparation Step 2: List the programs you will need again

After a clean install, most programs must be installed again.

Make a simple list:

- Office software (Word, Excel)

- PDF reader

- Browser you prefer

- Antivirus (if you plan to use one)

- Any special software for work

Also gather the installers if you have them, or at least note the program names so you can find them later.

Preparation Step 3: Collect your drivers or at least your network driver

Drivers are what allow Windows to talk to your hardware.

After installing Windows, the biggest frustration is:

"No internet."

That usually happens because the network driver is missing.

So before you install or upgrade:

- identify your network adapter (wired and wireless)

- download the correct drivers from the computer manufacturer if possible

- save them on a USB flash drive

If you do not know how to do that, do not panic. Many Windows installs detect drivers automatically. But you should still prepare, especially for older laptops.

Preparation Step 4: Check your disk space and system health

Before upgrading, you want enough disk space and a stable system.

Do this quick check:

1. Click Start.

2. Click Computer.

3. Look at Local Disk (C:).

You should have free space available. If the disk is almost full, an upgrade may fail, or Windows may run poorly.

Also, if your computer is already crashing, freezing, or infected, upgrading may carry the problems into the new system. In that case, a clean install is usually better, but only after backup.

Preparation Step 5: Confirm your Windows edition goal

Ask yourself a direct question:

"What edition do I need after installation?"

Use this simple guide:

- If you only need basic home use: Home is often enough.

- If you need office features and stronger control: Professional is usually best.

- If you want every feature and you know you will use advanced tools: Ultimate.

Also remember:

Installing a higher edition does not automatically fix slow hardware. A weak PC stays weak.

Preparation Step 6: Gather your product key (if needed)

Some installations require a product key during setup or later during activation.

If your PC came with Windows 7 installed, the key may be:

- on a sticker on the laptop bottom or inside the battery area

- in documentation that came with the computer

- tied to your installation media and packaging

Write it down carefully if you have it.

Preparation Step 7: Plan your upgrade path honestly

Before upgrading, decide which of these you are doing:

- Upgrade install (keeping files and programs where possible)

- Clean install (erase and install fresh)

A clean install is often the best way to remove long-term problems, but it requires strong backup discipline.

An upgrade is easier, but if the old system has issues, the new one may still feel messy.

You will make this decision in the next chapters, but start thinking about it now.

Try it now

[TRY IT NOW] Identify your Windows 7 edition and system type

1. Click Start.

2. Right-click Computer.

3. Click Properties.

4. Write down:

    o   Windows edition

    o   System type (32-bit or 64-bit)

    o   Installed memory (RAM)

If you want to be extra sure, also run:

- Start > type winver > Enter

Write down what you see.

Quick checklist before you move to Chapter Two

- I know my Windows 7 edition (Starter, Home, Professional, or Ultimate).

- I know if my system is 32-bit or 64-bit.

- I know my RAM size.

- I have a plan to back up my files before any install or upgrade.

- I understand that edition affects features, not speed.

CHAPTER TWO: GETTING A LEGITIMATE COPY AND PREPARING INSTALLATION MEDIA

Before you install or upgrade Windows 7, you need two things to be true:

1. You must have a legitimate Windows 7 license (a real product key that is allowed to activate Windows).

2. You must have reliable installation media (DVD or USB) that matches your edition and system type.

If either one is missing, the process can turn into frustration fast. Many beginners end up installing a modified copy from the internet, then discover later that it is infected, unstable, or cannot activate. This chapter helps you avoid those traps and prepare the safe, correct way.

Where Windows 7 normally comes from (preinstalled vs. media)

Windows 7 usually reaches users in one of these ways:

- Preinstalled on a computer (often called OEM)

- Bought as a boxed copy or download (often called Retail)

- Provided through a workplace or school program (volume licensing)

Let's break each one down in simple terms.

1) Preinstalled Windows 7 (OEM)

Many Windows 7 computers were sold with Windows already installed. In that case:

- The license is tied to that computer.

- The product key may be printed on a sticker (often under the laptop, inside the battery area, or on the desktop case).

- The computer may have a recovery partition that can reinstall Windows without a DVD.

Important things to know about preinstalled Windows:

- The edition matters. If your sticker says "Windows 7 Home Prem OA," then your computer is licensed for Windows 7 Home Premium, not Professional or Ultimate.

- The key is meant for that PC. It is usually not legally transferable to a different computer.

- Some manufacturers shipped recovery DVDs, but many did not. Instead, they expected you to create recovery discs yourself.

[TIP] If your computer originally came with Windows 7, look for a sticker called "Certificate of Authenticity" (COA). It usually includes the edition and a product key. Keep it safe.

[WARNING] If the COA sticker is damaged or unreadable, do not guess the key. You may need to use other methods to recover the key if Windows is still running, or use manufacturer recovery options.

2) Purchased Windows 7 (Retail)

A retail copy was bought separately, often in a box, or as a downloadable purchase back when Windows 7 was sold widely.

Retail copies are usually:

- Easier to reinstall on the same PC

- Sometimes transferable to another PC (depending on the license terms)

- More flexible than OEM

Retail copies usually include:

- A product key on a card or box label

- Installation media (DVD), or a way to download an ISO file

[TIP] If you have a retail box, do not throw it away. That box and key are often the difference between "easy reinstall" and "stuck."

3) Workplace or school Windows 7 (Volume)

Some Windows 7 installations were provided by organizations. In that case:

- Activation may be handled through the organization's IT tools.

- The key might not be printed anywhere for the user.

- Reinstalling later without IT support can be difficult.

If you received Windows 7 this way, the safest path is to talk to the organization that provided it, or plan for a different Windows version if that is the only practical option.

What "legitimate" really means (and what it does not mean)

A legitimate Windows 7 copy means:

- You have a valid license for the edition you are installing.

- The installation files have not been altered by unknown people.

- The system can activate normally using legitimate activation methods.

A legitimate copy does NOT mean:

- "It works without asking for a key."

- "It is activated by a crack."

- "It came from a random download link."

[WARNING] Avoid activators, cracks, and "pre-activated" Windows downloads. Even if they appear to work, they commonly come with malware, hidden tools, or unstable system changes that later cause crashes, missing updates, strange pop-ups, or stolen passwords.

Matching the right edition and system type before you create media

Before you make a DVD or USB installer, confirm two things from Chapter One:

- Edition: Starter, Home, Professional, Ultimate

- System type: 32-bit or 64-bit

Why matching matters:

- If you install the wrong edition, your key may not activate.

- If you install the wrong system type, some drivers may fail, and some programs may not work.

[NOTE] Windows 7 Starter is usually found on certain low-power machines. It is not commonly installed from standard retail DVDs. Many Starter machines used manufacturer recovery.

[TRY IT NOW] Confirm your edition and system type again

- Start
- Right-click Computer
- Properties
- Write down edition and system type

Backup checklist before you change anything

Most beginners only learn the value of backups after losing something. You should treat backup as part of installation, not as an extra step you might skip.

This is the safest backup checklist for Windows 7 install or upgrade.

[CHECKLIST] Files and folders you should back up

Personal files (most important)

- Documents folder
- Desktop folder
- Pictures folder
- Music folder
- Videos folder
- Downloads folder (only if it contains things you cannot re-download)

Work files

- Any custom work folders you created on C:
- Any project folders on D: (if you are not sure whether D: will be affected)

Browser data

- Bookmarks/Favorites
- Saved passwords (if you rely on them)
- Important saved autofill info (if you use it for work)

Email and contacts (if you use desktop email programs)

- Outlook PST files or profile exports
- Thunderbird profile backups if relevant

Application data that people forget

- Templates you created in Word or other editors
- Accounting files
- Password manager vault (export or backup file if needed)
- Notes stored locally

Drivers (optional but smart)

- Network driver installer (Wi-Fi and Ethernet) saved to USB

[TIP] The Desktop folder is easy to forget. Many people store important things on the Desktop. Back it up as if it is a second Documents folder.

[CHECKLIST] What to write down before you reinstall

Even if you back up files, write down these details:

- Your Windows 7 edition

- Your product key (if you have it)

- Your main installed programs you will need again

- Your Wi-Fi network name and password (if you do not know it by heart)

- Your printer model name (if you use a printer)

If the computer is old and drivers are hard to find later, also write down:

- Laptop/desktop brand and model number

- Network adapter type if you can find it (Device Manager can show it)

[STEP] A simple, safe backup method for beginners

1. Plug in an external drive or USB drive with enough space.

2. Create a folder on the external drive named: Backup Before Windows 7 Changes

3. Copy these folders from your PC into it: Documents, Desktop, Pictures, Music, Videos

4. Copy any extra work folders you created outside those.

5. Open a few copied files from the external drive to confirm they open.

[WARNING] Do not assume the copy worked. Always test by opening at least 3 to 5 files from the backup drive.

[TRY IT NOW] Test your backup

- Open your external drive.

- Open the backup folder.

- Open one document, one photo, and one PDF or other file.

- Confirm they open normally.

If they open, your backup is real.

Boot options basics (DVD or USB)

After you have a legitimate Windows 7 installer, you still need one more skill:

You must be able to boot from the installation media.

Boot means: the computer starts from the DVD or USB instead of starting from the hard drive where Windows currently lives.

If you do not boot from the media, you will not reach the Windows setup screen. Instead, the computer will start the old Windows again, and you will think the installer is "not working."

Let's make this simple.

What happens during boot (simple explanation)

When you press the power button, the computer checks for boot devices in a certain order. A common order is:

1. Hard drive (current Windows)

2. DVD drive

3. USB drive

4. Network boot (in some systems)

If the hard drive is first, it will load the old Windows before checking DVD or USB.

So you either:

- change the boot order in BIOS/UEFI settings, or

- use a one-time Boot Menu key to choose DVD or USB for that startup

For beginners, the Boot Menu method is usually easier and safer.

DVD installation media basics

A Windows 7 DVD installer is a disc that contains the setup files.

You can use it if:

- your computer has a working DVD drive
- the DVD is not scratched or damaged
- the computer can boot from DVD

How to boot from DVD (general method)

1. Insert the Windows 7 DVD.
2. Restart the computer.
3. Watch the screen carefully for a message like:
"Press any key to boot from CD or DVD…"
4. Press a key quickly (Spacebar is fine).

If you miss the moment, it will boot normally into Windows. Restart and try again.

[COMMON PROBLEM] "I inserted the DVD, but it still starts Windows."

This usually means one of these:

- You did not press a key when prompted.
- The computer is not set to check DVD before hard drive.
- The DVD drive is not working.
- The DVD is not bootable.

Solution:

- Try the Boot Menu key method (explained below).
- If the DVD drive is unreliable, use USB instead.

USB installation media basics

USB installation media means you have a bootable USB flash drive that contains Windows 7 setup files.

USB is often better than DVD because:

- it installs faster

- many modern laptops do not have DVD drives

- it is less likely to fail due to scratches

But USB has one key requirement:

It must be bootable.

Copying Windows files onto a USB drive is not always enough. The USB must be prepared in a way that the computer can boot from it.

[WARNING] Many "Windows USB" drives sold in informal markets are modified or unsafe. Only use USB media you trust or that you created yourself from trusted files.

Boot Menu keys (the easiest method for most users)

Most computers have a Boot Menu key you can press during startup. This shows a list of devices, like:

- Hard drive

- CD/DVD

- USB

- Network

You choose DVD or USB, and the computer boots from it for that startup only.

Common Boot Menu keys include:

- F12 (very common on Dell, Lenovo, many others)

- F9 (common on HP)

- Esc (sometimes opens a menu that leads to boot options)

- F8, F10, or F11 on some systems

[NOTE] The exact key depends on the manufacturer. The key is often shown briefly on the startup screen, like:
"Press F12 for Boot Menu"

[STEP] How to use the Boot Menu

1. Insert your Windows 7 DVD or plug in your Windows 7 USB.

2. Restart the computer.

3. As soon as the first logo appears, start tapping the Boot Menu key repeatedly. Do not hold it down. Tap it.

4. When the Boot Menu appears, choose:

    o   USB Storage Device, or

    o   Removable Device, or

    o   CD/DVD Drive

5. Press Enter.

If the media is correct, Windows setup will start.

[COMMON PROBLEM] "I pressed F12 but nothing happened."

Fixes:

- Restart and tap earlier, right after powering on.

- Try a different key (F9, Esc, F10).

- If using a wireless keyboard, use a wired keyboard for this step.

- Some laptops require you to press Fn + F12.

BIOS boot order (when Boot Menu does not work)

BIOS settings control hardware startup behavior. You can change the boot order so that DVD or USB is checked before the hard drive.

This method is more permanent, so be careful.

[WARNING] Do not change settings you do not understand.

In BIOS, one wrong change can cause boot failure. If you only need to boot once from DVD/USB, Boot Menu is the safer choice.

[STEP] General BIOS boot order method

1. Restart the computer.

2. Press the BIOS setup key repeatedly at startup.
   Common keys: Del, F2, F10

3. Look for "Boot" or "Boot Order."

4. Move USB or CD/DVD above the hard drive.

5. Save and exit.

Then the computer will attempt DVD/USB first each time until you change it back.

[TIP] If you use this method, set it back after installation so normal startup is smooth.

Choosing between DVD and USB: what beginners should do

Use DVD if:

- your DVD drive works well

- you already have a clean, trusted Windows 7 DVD

- you are comfortable using "Press any key to boot from CD/DVD"

Use USB if:

- your laptop has no DVD drive

- your DVD drive is weak or unreliable

- you want a faster installation

- you want to keep installation media that does not scratch

For many users today, USB is the better option.

Final preparation checklist before you move to installation

Before you touch the install button, confirm these items:

[CHECKLIST]

- I have a legitimate Windows 7 license or key for the edition I plan to install.

- I know whether I need 32-bit or 64-bit.

- My files are backed up and tested.

- I know how I will boot the computer (DVD or USB).

- I can access the Boot Menu key or BIOS if needed.

- I have a plan for drivers, especially network drivers.

[TRY IT NOW] Practice: boot test without installing yet

You can test whether your DVD/USB boots without starting the installation process fully.

1. Insert DVD or plug in USB.

2. Restart.

3. Open Boot Menu and select DVD/USB.

4. Wait for the Windows setup screen to appear.

5. When it appears, do not click Install yet.

6. Shut down or restart and remove the media.

If you can reach the setup screen, your media and boot method are working.

That one test saves hours of stress later.

CHAPTER THREE: INSTALLING WINDOWS 7 STEP BY STEP

This chapter walks you through a clean Windows 7 installation from the moment you press the power button to the moment you reach your first usable desktop. A clean installation means you install Windows fresh. It is the most reliable method, especially if your computer has been slow, infected, unstable, or filled with old clutter.

A clean install can feel intimidating to beginners because it involves choices about disks, partitions, and settings. But if you follow the steps carefully and read the warnings, you can do it safely.

Before you begin, confirm two things from Chapter Two:

- Your important files are backed up and tested.

- Your installation media boots correctly (DVD or USB).

If those two are true, you are ready.

Clean installation flow: from start to first login

Step 1: Insert the Windows 7 DVD or plug in the USB

- If you are installing from DVD, insert it first, then restart the PC.

- If you are installing from USB, plug it in first, then restart.

[TIP] Plug the USB directly into the computer, not into a hub. Some hubs cause boot problems.

Step 2: Boot from the installation media

Restart the computer and use one of these methods:

- Boot Menu method (best for beginners)
- BIOS boot order method (only if Boot Menu fails)

If using DVD, you may see:
"Press any key to boot from CD or DVD…"

Press any key quickly (Spacebar works).

If using USB, you may simply see the installer start after selecting USB in the Boot Menu.

If Windows starts normally instead of the installer, you did not boot from the media. Restart and try again.

Step 3: Wait for "Windows is loading files…"

If the installer is booting, you will see:

- "Windows is loading files…"
- A progress bar
- Then the Windows 7 setup screen with language options

Be patient. On older computers, this can take several minutes.

Step 4: Choose language, time, and keyboard settings

You will see a screen asking:

- Language to install
- Time and currency format
- Keyboard or input method

Most people leave these on the default.

[NOTE] Choose the keyboard layout you actually use. If you choose the wrong one, typing can feel strange later.

Click Next.

Step 5: Click "Install now"

Click Install now.

Setup will begin preparing.

You may see a checkbox about getting updates for installation. If the computer has no internet yet, it is fine. You can update later.

Step 6: Accept the license terms

Check "I accept the license terms" and click Next.

Step 7: Choose installation type

You will see two options:

- Upgrade
- Custom (advanced)

For a clean installation, choose:
Custom (advanced)

This does not mean you are an advanced user. It simply means you are installing fresh rather than upgrading.

The most important step: choosing where to install Windows

This is the step where beginners must slow down. It is where most mistakes happen.

You will see a list of partitions. A partition is a section of a hard drive. Your computer may show:

- Disk 0 Partition 1
- Disk 0 Partition 2
- "System Reserved"
- A partition labeled "Recovery"
- Unallocated Space

What you see depends on your computer's history.

Understanding common partition names

- System Reserved: a small partition Windows uses for boot files.
- Recovery: a manufacturer partition that can restore the computer to factory state.
- Primary: where Windows is usually installed.
- Unallocated Space: empty area where no partition exists yet.

[WARNING] If you delete or format the wrong partition, you can lose data or manufacturer recovery options. Only proceed if your backups are complete.

Choosing your clean install approach (safe options for beginners)

There are two common clean-install approaches:

Option A: Install Windows without deleting all partitions (safer)

This option is safer if you are not sure what each partition is.

You choose the main partition (often the largest one) and install Windows there. Setup may move the old Windows into a folder called Windows.old.

Benefits:

- Less risk of deleting recovery partitions accidentally

- Easier for beginners

Downside:

- Some old clutter may remain in Windows.old (but it is not active Windows)

Option B: Delete partitions and install into unallocated space (full reset)

This option gives the cleanest result, but it is more dangerous if you do not understand partitions.

Benefits:

- Freshest possible install
- Removes old junk and partitions

Downside:

- Can delete recovery partition
- Can erase everything completely

If you are a beginner, Option A is usually the best starting point unless you specifically want a full wipe.

Step 8: Select the target partition

To choose where Windows installs:

1. Click the partition that you want to install Windows on.
2. Look at the size and free space.

Usually, the correct target is the largest primary partition, often labeled something like:

- Disk 0 Partition 2 (Primary)

If you see "Drive options (advanced)," you can:

- Format

- Delete
- Create partitions

[WARNING] Formatting erases data on that partition. Do not format unless you are sure your backup is complete and you chose the correct partition.

For beginners, a practical safe approach is:

- Select the main partition
- Click Next
- Let Windows handle it

If Windows warns you that files might be moved to Windows.old, that is normal.

Step 9: Wait while Windows installs

Windows setup will:

- Copy Windows files
- Expand files
- Install features
- Install updates (sometimes)
- Complete installation

The computer may restart several times. This is normal.

[IMPORTANT] Do not press any key during restart when the "Press any key to boot from CD/DVD" message appears again. If you press a key, it will restart setup from the beginning.

Best habit:

- When the first restart happens, remove the DVD or USB, or leave it inserted but do not press any key. Some people remove the media to avoid confusion.

Step 10: First login setup (initial setup choices)

After installation, Windows will ask you for first-time setup choices. These settings shape your daily use.

Take them seriously, but do not fear them. You can change most of them later.

Initial setup choices: user account, computer name, basic settings

Step 11: Create a user account and computer name

Windows will ask:

- Type a user name

- Type a computer name

User name

This is the main account you will use daily. Choose something simple like:

- John
- Office
- Family
- Your real name

Avoid very long names or symbols.

Computer name

Windows creates a computer name based on your user name. This matters most for networks and sharing.

A good computer name is:

- short
- simple
- easy to recognize

Example:

- JOHN-PC

- OFFICE-LAPTOP

- HOME7

[TIP] If you plan to connect to networks, name the computer something you can recognize quickly.

Click Next.

Step 12: Create a password (recommended)

Windows will ask you to create a password.

You may see:

- Password

- Re-enter password

- Password hint

Use a password if your computer contains personal files or if other people can access it.

A good password is:

- something you can remember

- not your name or birth year

- not "12345" or "password"

A password hint should help you remember but should not reveal the password.

[WARNING] If you forget your password and have no recovery method, you can lock yourself out. Choose something you can remember.

Click Next.

Step 13: Enter the product key (activation)

Windows may ask for a product key.

You may also see a checkbox:
"Automatically activate Windows when I'm online"

If you have the key, enter it carefully.

If you do not have it right now, you can sometimes skip and enter later, depending on the media.

[NOTE] If you skip activation, Windows may still install but will later ask you to activate.

Step 14: Choose Windows Update settings

Windows will ask how you want updates handled.

Options often include:

- Use recommended settings

- Install important updates only

- Ask me later

For most users, choose:
Use recommended settings

Updates protect your computer and improve stability.

[WARNING] Windows 7 is an older system. Updates are critical for security. If you plan to use Windows 7, you must take updates seriously.

Step 15: Set time zone and date/time

Choose the correct time zone and confirm the date/time.

Wrong time can cause:

- update errors
- browser certificate issues
- confusion in file timestamps

Click Next.

Step 16: Choose your network location (Home, Work, Public)

If Windows detects a network, it may ask:

- Home network

- Work network
- Public network

Choose carefully:

Home network:

- best for your own private home Wi-Fi
- allows easier sharing and discovery

Work network:

- for office networks
- more controlled, but still allows some networking

Public network:

- for cafés, airports, hotels
- safest, blocks many sharing features

[TIP] If you are not sure, choose Public. You can change it later.

Step 17: Reach the desktop (first login complete)

Windows will finalize settings and take you to the desktop.

This is your first usable Windows 7 session.

Now the real work begins: making the system stable, connected, and ready.

First tasks after installation: drivers, basic updates, essential apps

Many beginners stop at "the desktop appeared" and assume the job is done. But a fresh Windows install is only the foundation. The computer may still be missing drivers, updates, and essential tools.

Your goal now is:

- get drivers installed
- get internet working
- update Windows
- install essential applications
- confirm the system is stable

Task 1: Check Device Manager for missing drivers

Drivers are the most common post-install problem.

[STEP] Open Device Manager

1. Click Start.

2. Right-click Computer.

3. Click Manage.

4. Click Device Manager.

Look for devices with:

- a yellow triangle
- a question mark
- "Unknown device"

Those signs mean the driver is missing.

Common missing drivers after Windows install:

- Network adapter (Wi-Fi)
- Graphics card (screen resolution stuck low)
- Audio device (no sound)
- Chipset driver (system stability and hardware detection)

[TIP] Fix network driver first. Once internet works, finding the rest becomes easier.

Task 2: Connect to the internet

If Wi-Fi works immediately, connect and proceed.

If Wi-Fi does not work:

- try Ethernet cable if possible (wired connection often works faster)

- install network driver from the USB you prepared earlier

- if you have the computer model, you can download drivers from the manufacturer on another computer

[COMMON PROBLEM] "No wireless networks appear."

Possible causes:

- Wi-Fi driver missing

- Wi-Fi switch on laptop is off

- function key (Fn + key) disables Wi-Fi

Fix:

- check Device Manager for missing network driver

- ensure Wi-Fi is enabled physically on the laptop if there is a switch

- try wired internet temporarily

Task 3: Run Windows Update (basic updates)

Once internet is working, update Windows.

[STEP] Run Windows Update

1. Click Start.

2. Click Control Panel.

3. Click System and Security.

4. Click Windows Update.

5. Click Check for updates.

6. Install important updates.

This can take time, especially on older systems. The first update cycle is usually the longest.

[TIP] Expect restarts. After each restart, return to Windows Update and check again until there are no more important updates.

Task 4: Install essential applications

A clean Windows install gives you a basic system. You may still need the tools you use daily.

Essential apps for most users:

- A browser you trust (if you do not want to rely on the default)

- A PDF reader

- Office software (or an alternative office suite)

- A media player (optional)

- Antivirus or security tool (if you plan to use one)

[WARNING] Avoid installing many "free cleaners" or "boosters." Focus on trusted software.

Task 5: Confirm screen resolution and sound

If your screen looks stretched or low quality:

- install graphics driver

- check Display settings after driver installation

If sound is missing:

- install audio driver

- check speaker volume and playback device

These two issues are common right after installation.

Task 6: Set up a simple file structure and restore your files

Once stable, you can copy your backed-up files back to the computer.

Recommended approach:

- Restore Documents first
- Restore Pictures next
- Restore work folders last

[TIP] Do not dump everything back onto the Desktop. Use Documents and organized folders. Your future self will thank you.

[TRY IT NOW] Post-install health check

Do these checks after you reach the desktop:

1. Open Device Manager and look for missing drivers.
2. Confirm Wi-Fi or Ethernet works.
3. Run Windows Update once.
4. Confirm sound works by playing a small audio file.
5. Confirm screen resolution looks correct.

6. Install at least one browser and a PDF reader.

7. Shut down and restart once to confirm it boots cleanly.

If all those are good, your installation is successful and stable.

CHAPTER FOUR: UPGRADING TO WINDOWS 7 SAFELY

A clean installation gives you the freshest possible Windows 7 system. An upgrade, on the other hand, tries to move you from an older Windows version into Windows 7 while keeping as much of your current setup as possible.

Both methods can work. Both methods can also fail if you choose the wrong one for your situation.

This chapter helps you make a smart choice, protect your files, and avoid the upgrade problems that trap beginners. The goal is simple:

Keep what matters, avoid surprises, and end up with a stable Windows 7 system you can trust.

Upgrade vs. clean install (when each makes sense)

Before you touch the installer, ask yourself one honest question:

Do I want Windows 7 to feel like a fresh start, or do I want it to feel like the same computer with a newer Windows?

That question points directly to the right method.

What an upgrade is

An upgrade install means you run the Windows 7 setup while your current Windows is still running. Setup tries to:

- keep your personal files

- keep user accounts

- keep many settings

- keep many installed programs

- replace the old Windows system files with Windows 7 system files

An upgrade aims for convenience.

But the convenience has a cost: if the old system is messy, some of that mess can move into the new system.

What a clean install is

A clean install means Windows 7 is installed fresh on the hard drive. You usually back up your files first, then install Windows 7 as a new system.

A clean install aims for stability.

It takes more effort, but the result is often faster and more reliable, especially for older computers that have been used for years without proper maintenance.

When an upgrade makes sense

Choose an upgrade if most of the following are true:

- Your current Windows is stable and not infected.

- Your computer starts normally and rarely crashes.

- You have many programs installed and you strongly want to keep them.

- You do not want to spend time reinstalling software and reconfiguring settings.

- You have enough free disk space.

- You are upgrading from a Windows version that supports a clean upgrade path to Windows 7.

[TIP] If your current Windows feels healthy, an upgrade can save time.

[NOTE] Even in an upgrade, you still must back up your files. An upgrade is not a backup.

When a clean install makes sense

Choose a clean install if any of these are true:

- Your computer is slow even after basic cleanup.

- You suspect malware or past infections.

- The system crashes, freezes, or shows strange errors often.

- Startup is very slow and has been slow for a long time.

- You want the best chance of a smooth Windows 7 experience.

- You do not mind reinstalling programs afterward.

- You want to change from 32-bit to 64-bit (this usually requires a clean install).

[WARNING] If your old system is unstable, an upgrade can carry instability into Windows 7.

A simple decision test (for beginners)

Answer these questions:

- Does the computer feel clean and stable today?

- Do I trust it enough to keep its installed programs and settings?

- Am I willing to reinstall programs if needed?

If you answered "no" to the first two, choose a clean install.

If you answered "yes" to the first two and "no" to reinstalling programs, try an upgrade.

What to keep and what to reinstall

Many beginners believe an upgrade keeps everything. That is not always true.

Think of an upgrade like moving to a new house with a moving truck. You can bring most furniture, but some items will not fit, and some items will break in the move.

This section helps you prepare for what will likely remain and what you should plan to reinstall.

What an upgrade often keeps

In many successful upgrades, Windows 7 will keep:

- your personal files (Documents, Pictures, Music, Desktop, etc.)

- your user accounts and passwords

- your basic settings (many Control Panel settings)

- many installed programs (especially common ones)

- many printers and devices (if drivers remain compatible)

- your network profiles (sometimes)

[NOTE] "Keeps" does not always mean "works perfectly." Some programs might remain installed but behave strangely until updated or repaired.

What an upgrade often does NOT keep perfectly

Even in a good upgrade, you should expect to reinstall or repair some things:

- older antivirus software (often needs removal or replacement)

- older drivers (especially graphics and network drivers)

- programs that deeply modify the system (disk tools, system cleaners, old firewall tools)

- some hardware utilities (touchpad tools, hotkey tools)

- some printer drivers (especially older models)

- certain older games and legacy applications

[TIP] If a program came from a CD years ago and has never been updated, plan to reinstall it.

What you should always back up, even if you are upgrading

Even when upgrading, back up these items as if you were doing a clean install:

- Documents

- Desktop

- Pictures

- any work folders you created outside the normal library folders

- browser bookmarks

- any password vault files or exported backups (if you use a password manager)

- email data if you use a desktop email program

[WARNING] If the upgrade fails, you may end up needing a clean install. Your backup is your safety net.

What you should always plan to reinstall after an upgrade

To avoid confusion and downtime, plan to reinstall these if needed:

- antivirus or security software (if the old one causes issues)
- graphics driver (if resolution looks wrong or performance is poor)
- audio driver (if sound is missing or distorted)
- network driver (if Wi-Fi disappears)
- printer drivers (if printing fails)

[CHECKLIST] Pre-upgrade "write it down" list

Before you upgrade, write down:

- your Windows edition and system type (32-bit or 64-bit)
- your key programs you cannot live without
- your printer model (if you use one)
- your Wi-Fi name and password

- your browser bookmarks export method (if you know it)

If you do this, you will not feel stuck if something goes missing.

How to upgrade to Windows 7 safely (step by step)

This is the safest beginner path for a typical upgrade scenario.

Important note: an upgrade is usually started from inside your current Windows. You do not boot from DVD/USB to start an in-place upgrade in the simplest method. Booting from media is often used for clean installs.

Step 1: Confirm that your current system is healthy enough to upgrade

Before you upgrade, do a basic health check:

- restart the computer once and confirm it boots normally
- run a quick antivirus scan if you have antivirus installed
- uninstall unknown toolbars or suspicious programs
- remove temporary files if disk space is low

[WARNING] If the system is infected, upgrading is a bad idea. Choose a clean install instead.

Step 2: Make your full backup

Use the backup checklist from Chapter Two. Then test the backup by opening a few files from the backup drive.

This step is not optional.

Step 3: Free up disk space

Upgrades need room to work. If the drive is too full, upgrades fail.

A safe minimum varies by system, but as a beginner rule:

Try to keep at least 20 GB free on the system drive (C:) before upgrading.

You can free space by:

- emptying Recycle Bin
- deleting temporary files
- moving large videos to an external drive
- uninstalling programs you no longer use

[TIP] If the drive is nearly full, a clean install with proper organization might be the better long-term fix.

Step 4: Disconnect unnecessary devices

During upgrade, keep only the essentials connected:

- keyboard and mouse
- monitor (for desktop PC)
- internet cable if needed

Unplug:

- extra USB drives
- external hard drives (except the one with your backup, and even that can be unplugged during upgrade)
- printers and scanners (they can be reconnected later)

This reduces driver conflicts during setup.

Step 5: Temporarily disable or uninstall certain security tools

Some older security tools interfere with Windows upgrades. If you have a heavy third-party security suite, consider:

- disabling it temporarily during the upgrade, or

- uninstalling it and reinstalling after Windows 7 is installed

[WARNING] Do not download random security tools during upgrade. Use trusted sources only, and reinstall after the system is stable.

Step 6: Start the upgrade from within Windows

1. Insert the Windows 7 DVD or connect the Windows 7 USB while your current Windows is running.

2. If setup starts automatically, choose "Install now."

3. If it does not start, open Computer, open the DVD/USB drive, and double-click setup.exe.

Windows 7 Setup will open.

Follow the prompts until you reach the choice:

- Upgrade

- Custom (advanced)

Choose: Upgrade

Step 7: Let setup check compatibility

Setup may scan your system and report:

- incompatible programs
- drivers that might not work
- actions you must take before continuing

If setup warns about a program, take it seriously. Remove the program if required, then restart and run setup again.

[TIP] When setup tells you to remove a program, it is often a security tool, an old driver utility, or a system modification tool.

Step 8: Complete the upgrade and stay patient

The system may reboot multiple times. This is normal.

Do not:

- force shutdown unless the system has clearly frozen for a very long time
- press keys that restart setup from DVD (if the DVD message appears during reboot)
- unplug the computer mid-upgrade

After the upgrade finishes, you will reach the Windows 7 login screen and then the desktop.

That is not the end. The post-upgrade tasks are where stability is earned.

After-upgrade tasks (the important finishing steps)

Once Windows 7 is running:

1. Check Device Manager for missing drivers.

2. Confirm internet works.

3. Run Windows Update and restart when required.

4. Test your sound.

5. Test screen resolution and graphics performance.

6. Open your key programs and confirm they run.

7. If a key program fails, repair or reinstall it.

8. Reconnect your printer and test printing.

[TIP] Do not install twenty things immediately. Stabilize first, then add software slowly.

Common upgrade problems and quick fixes

Upgrades fail for predictable reasons. This section lists the most common issues and what beginners can do quickly before panic sets in.

Problem 1: The "Upgrade" option is not available

Sometimes setup only offers "Custom (advanced)."

Common causes:

- you are trying to start setup by booting from DVD/USB instead of running setup.exe inside Windows

- your current Windows version does not support an in-place upgrade to that Windows 7 edition

- the installer does not match your system type (32-bit vs 64-bit)

Quick fixes:

- start setup from inside your current Windows using setup.exe

- confirm you are using the correct 32-bit or 64-bit installer

- if your system path does not support upgrade, choose a clean install and restore files from backup

[NOTE] A clean install is not a failure. It is often the better result.

Problem 2: "Not enough disk space"

Setup may stop and demand more space.

Quick fixes:

- empty Recycle Bin
- remove temporary files
- uninstall unused programs
- move large personal files to an external drive temporarily

Then restart setup.

Problem 3: Upgrade freezes or seems stuck

This is scary for beginners because it looks like nothing is happening.

What to do first:

- wait longer than you think you should, especially on older computers

- watch the hard drive activity light (if it is blinking, work is happening)

If it has clearly frozen for a long time and shows no activity:

- restart only as a last resort
- after restart, setup may resume or roll back automatically

If it rolls back:

- remove incompatible programs (especially security tools)
- unplug extra devices
- try again, or choose a clean install

Problem 4: Endless reboot loop after upgrade attempt

The computer restarts repeatedly and never reaches the desktop.

Quick fixes:

- unplug DVD/USB and restart (to prevent restarting setup)
- try the Advanced Boot Options menu:

- restart the computer

- tap F8 repeatedly before Windows starts

- choose "Last Known Good Configuration" if available

- or choose "Safe Mode" if it loads

If Safe Mode loads:

- uninstall recently installed drivers or tools

- remove incompatible programs

- restart normally

If nothing loads:

- use "Repair your computer" from the Windows 7 DVD/USB to run Startup Repair

- if repair fails, plan a clean install and restore files from backup

[WARNING] When you see repeated boot loops, do not keep forcing restarts many times. Use repair tools or shift to a clean install plan.

Problem 5: No internet after upgrade

Wi-Fi disappears or network will not connect.

Quick fixes:

- restart once

- open Device Manager and check the network adapter

- if the adapter shows a warning symbol, install the correct driver

- if possible, use a wired Ethernet connection temporarily

- run Windows Update after connection is restored, because it may fetch drivers

Problem 6: No sound after upgrade

Quick fixes:

- check the volume icon and confirm it is not muted

- right-click the volume icon and choose Playback devices

- set the correct speakers as default

- install or reinstall the audio driver from the manufacturer if needed

Problem 7: Screen looks stretched or stuck at low resolution

This usually means the graphics driver is missing or old.

Quick fixes:

- install the correct graphics driver
- restart after driver install
- then set proper resolution in Screen Resolution settings

Problem 8: Programs "disappeared" or no longer work

Some programs may not survive the upgrade.

Quick fixes:

- search the Start menu for the program name
- check Control Panel > Programs and Features to see if it is installed
- if installed but broken, repair it from its installer or uninstall and reinstall
- if not installed, reinstall it from your original installer or trusted source

[TIP] If a program is important for work, test it early, not weeks later.

Problem 9: Activation problems after upgrade

Windows may say it is not activated or the key is invalid.

Quick fixes:

- confirm you installed the edition that matches your product key

- re-enter the key carefully (most mistakes are typing errors)

- ensure the computer date and time are correct

- connect to the internet and try activation again

If the edition does not match your key:

- you may need to reinstall the correct edition, or use the correct key for the installed edition

[WARNING] Avoid unofficial activation tools. If your license does not match, fix the edition or the license, not the system integrity.

Problem 10: Windows Update fails repeatedly after upgrade

This can happen on older systems or after upgrades.

Quick fixes:

- restart and try again

- run Windows Update in smaller batches (install important updates first, restart, repeat)

- ensure date and time are correct

- check that internet is stable

If updates remain stubborn:

- prioritize installing the most critical updates first

- keep the system stable before installing extra software

[TRY IT NOW] Upgrade readiness test

Before you commit to the upgrade, do this short test:

- Backup completed and tested: yes or no

- Free disk space above 20 GB: yes or no

- Unnecessary devices unplugged: yes or no

- Antivirus tool plan (disable or uninstall temporarily): yes or no

- Windows 7 installer matches 32-bit or 64-bit: yes or no

- You can run setup.exe from inside current Windows: yes or no

If you answered "no" to any item, fix it first. That is how safe upgrades happen.

The big rule of safe upgrades

A safe upgrade is not about luck. It is about preparation.

If you back up properly, match the correct installer, remove conflicting tools, and stay patient during setup, you can upgrade successfully.

If the upgrade fails, do not treat it as the end. A clean install with your backup restored is often the path that gives the best long-term result.

PART TWO: DAILY USE SKILLS (THE FEATURES PEOPLE TOUCH EVERY DAY)

Windows 7 becomes easy when you master three areas that you use every single time you sit at a computer:

1. The desktop (where you land after you sign in)

2. The Start menu (where you find programs and settings fast)

3. The taskbar (where you switch between what you are doing)

Many beginners struggle not because Windows is complicated, but because they do not have a simple routine for finding things and moving between tasks. This chapter builds that routine.

CHAPTER FIVE: THE DESKTOP, START MENU, AND TASKBAR

The big idea of this chapter

Your goal is not to memorize everything on the screen. Your goal is to build three habits:

- Keep the desktop clean so you can think clearly.

- Use Start menu search instead of hunting with your eyes.

- Use the taskbar as your control center for switching, not as a messy parking lot.

When you do those three, Windows 7 feels calm and predictable.

1) Desktop basics and icons

What the desktop really is

The desktop is a workspace. It is not a storage room.

Beginners often use the desktop as their main folder and drop everything there. That works for a few days, then it becomes a pile. A piled desktop leads to:

- losing files

- opening the wrong version of a document

- feeling stressed every time you log in

A better approach is:

- Keep only shortcuts on the desktop.

- Keep real files inside Documents and organized folders.

Shortcuts are safe because if you delete a shortcut, you usually do not delete the real file.

Common desktop parts you should recognize

On a typical Windows 7 desktop, you may see:

- Desktop icons (small pictures you click)
- The taskbar at the bottom
- The Recycle Bin icon
- A desktop background (wallpaper)

You may also see gadgets on the side (a clock, weather, etc.). Those are optional.

What an icon can represent

Not every icon is the same. In Windows 7, an icon can be:

1. A program shortcut (opens an app)
2. A folder shortcut (opens a folder)
3. A real file (opens a document, photo, or video)
4. A system tool (Recycle Bin, Computer, Control Panel)

How to tell a shortcut from a real file:

- Most shortcuts have a small arrow on the icon.

- A real file usually shows the file type icon (Word, PDF, image, etc.) and often has a file extension (if extensions are visible).

[TIP] If you want a clean desktop, keep shortcuts, not real files.

The Recycle Bin: what it does and what it does not do

The Recycle Bin is a safety net. When you delete many items, they go to the Recycle Bin first.

That means:

- You can restore deleted items if you deleted them by mistake.

- You can empty the Recycle Bin to free space.

But the Recycle Bin is not magic. Some deletions skip it, such as:

- deleting from some external drives

- using certain delete methods that permanently delete

- very large files that Windows decides not to store in the bin

[WARNING] Before emptying the Recycle Bin, quickly scan what is inside. People often delete something important by accident, then empty it and regret it.

Right-click: the fastest skill on the desktop

Right-clicking gives you power. On the desktop, right-click opens a menu with options such as:

- View (icon size and arrangement)
- Sort by (name, size, date)
- Refresh (fixes display issues)
- Paste (put copied items here)
- New (create folders and files)
- Screen resolution (display settings)
- Personalize (themes and background)

If you learn only one mouse habit, learn this:

Use right-click when you feel stuck.

Arranging icons (so the desktop stays usable)

If your icons are messy, do this:

[STEP]

1. Right-click an empty area on the desktop.
2. Click View.
3. Choose one:

    - Medium icons (good for most people)
    - Small icons (good for many icons)
    - Large icons (good for visibility)

Then:

[STEP]

1. Right-click an empty area again.
2. Click Sort by.
3. Choose Name to organize alphabetically.

Optional:

[STEP]

1. Right-click an empty area.
2. Click View.

3. Click Auto arrange icons if you want Windows to keep them in a grid.

[TIP] Auto arrange icons is helpful for beginners because icons do not drift around randomly.

Creating a folder on the desktop (for temporary work)

Sometimes you do need a folder on the desktop, especially for short projects.

[STEP]

1. Right-click an empty area on the desktop.

2. Click New.

3. Click Folder.

4. Type a name and press Enter.

Good folder names:

- Practice
- Today Work
- To Print
- Photos To Sort

[NOTE] If a folder is for long-term storage, move it into Documents later.

Creating a shortcut on the desktop (the right way)

If you open a program daily, create a shortcut instead of searching for it every time.

Method A: Send to Desktop

[STEP]

1. Click Start.
2. Find the program in All Programs (or search it).
3. Right-click the program.
4. Click Send to.
5. Click Desktop (create shortcut).

Method B: Create shortcut to a folder

[STEP]

1. Open Computer or Windows Explorer.
2. Find the folder you want.
3. Right-click the folder.

4. Click Send to.

5. Click Desktop (create shortcut).

Now your desktop stays clean but useful.

Showing important system icons (Computer, Control Panel, etc.)

If your desktop feels "empty" and you want quick access to system tools:

[STEP]

1. Right-click the desktop.

2. Click Personalize.

3. On the left, click Change desktop icons.

4. Tick what you want:

    o Computer

    o Control Panel

    o Network

    o User's Files

    o Recycle Bin

5. Click OK.

This is optional, but many beginners find it easier than hunting inside menus.

2) Start menu search habits (the fastest way to find anything)

Why Start menu search matters

Beginners often scroll through All Programs and lose time. Search is faster because you only type a few letters.

If you learn Start menu search, you can find:

- programs
- Control Panel tools
- settings
- files
- printers
- sometimes even help topics

Your new habit is:

Click Start, type, press Enter.

The Start menu layout in simple terms

When you click Start, you usually see:

- A left column: programs (recent and pinned)

- A right column: common places (Documents, Pictures, Computer, Control Panel)

- A search box at the bottom

The search box is the real tool. Use it.

How to search for programs

[STEP]

1. Press the Windows key on your keyboard (or click Start).

2. Type the program name.

3. When the program appears at the top, press Enter.

Examples to try:

- notepad

- calculator

- paint

- wordpad

- cmd (Command Prompt)
- control panel

[TIP] You do not need to type the full name. Just type enough letters.

How to search for settings and tools

Start menu search also finds Control Panel tools.

Examples:

- mouse (opens mouse settings)
- keyboard (opens keyboard settings)
- sound (opens sound settings)
- firewall (opens Windows Firewall)
- update (opens Windows Update)
- device manager (opens Device Manager)

[NOTE] If the result list shows many items, look at the category labels. Windows often groups results by Programs, Control Panel, and Documents.

How to search for your own files

Start menu search can find documents and folders, especially if they are in your Libraries (Documents, Pictures, etc.).

[STEP]

1. Press the Windows key.

2. Type part of the file name.

3. Look under Documents or Files.

Example:
If you have a file named "Budget 2026", type: budget

Windows will show likely matches.

[COMMON PROBLEM] "Search does not find my file."

Quick causes:

- The file name is different than you remember.

- The file is on an external drive that is not connected.

- Indexing has not included that folder yet.

Quick fixes:

- Try searching inside the folder where you think the file is.

- Use Windows Explorer search (top-right search box in a folder window).

- If you often store files in unusual folders, consider moving them into Documents.

Pinning items to the Start menu (for daily tools)

If you open the same program daily, pin it.

[STEP]

1. Click Start.

2. Find the program (search or All Programs).

3. Right-click it.

4. Click Pin to Start Menu.

Now it stays near the top, so you do not have to search every time.

To unpin:

[STEP]

1. Right-click the pinned program.

2. Click Unpin from Start Menu.

A simple Start menu routine (beginner-friendly)

Use this routine daily:

- Use Start search for programs.
- Pin only your top 5 to 10 programs.
- Do not pin everything.
- Use the right column for quick access to Documents and Control Panel.

A Start menu crowded with pinned items becomes as messy as a crowded desktop.

3) Taskbar pinning and switching between apps

What the taskbar is for

The taskbar is the strip along the bottom of the screen (unless moved). It has three jobs:

1. Launch programs fast (pinned icons)
2. Show what is currently open (active windows)
3. Let you switch between open windows quickly

If you learn the taskbar, you stop wasting time searching for windows that are already open.

Parts of the taskbar you should recognize

From left to right, you may see:

- Start button
- Pinned program icons
- Buttons for open programs
- Notification area (system tray) with clock, volume, network icon
- Show Desktop button at the far right (a small rectangle)

Pinning programs to the taskbar (best daily shortcut)

Pin the programs you use daily:

- your browser
- file explorer
- Word or your writing tool
- PDF reader
- email tool (if you use one)

[STEP]
Method A (from Start menu):

1. Click Start.
2. Find the program.
3. Right-click it.
4. Click Pin to Taskbar.

Method B (from an open program):

1. Open the program.
2. Right-click its taskbar icon.
3. Click Pin this program to taskbar.

To unpin:

- Right-click the icon and click Unpin this program from taskbar.

[TIP] Keep your taskbar pins limited. Too many pins reduce speed.

Switching between open programs (the easy ways)

Method A: Click the taskbar button

- If a program is open, click its icon on the taskbar.

- If the program has multiple windows, Windows may show small previews.

Method B: Alt + Tab (the classic switch)

- Hold Alt, press Tab.

- Keep pressing Tab to cycle.

- Release Alt to switch.

This is one of the most useful keyboard skills in Windows.

Method C: Windows key shortcuts for pinned apps
If you pin programs to the taskbar, Windows gives you a powerful shortcut:

- Windows key + 1 opens the first pinned app

- Windows key + 2 opens the second pinned app

- Windows key + 3 opens the third pinned app

If the program is already open, it switches to it.

Example:
If your browser is the first pinned icon, Windows key + 1 takes you there instantly.

[TIP] This is one of the fastest habits for writers and office users.

Using Jump Lists (quick access to recent files)

Windows 7 taskbar icons can show a "Jump List." This list often includes:

- recent documents
- frequent websites (for browsers)
- common tasks

[STEP]

1. Right-click a taskbar icon (example: Word, Excel, browser).
2. Look at the list of recent items.
3. Click an item to open it quickly.

[WARNING] If you share a computer, Jump Lists can show your recent files. Be mindful of privacy.

Using the Show Desktop button (instant clean view)

At the far right end of the taskbar is a small blank rectangle. That is the Show Desktop button.

- Click it to minimize everything and show the desktop.

- Click it again to bring windows back.

This is useful when you need a file on the desktop or you want a quick reset.

Taskbar settings that help beginners

Right-click an empty part of the taskbar, then click Properties.

Useful settings:

- Lock the taskbar
  Keeps it from moving by accident.

- Auto-hide the taskbar
  Hides it until you move the mouse to the bottom. Some people like it on small screens.

- Use small icons
  Saves space on small screens.

- Taskbar buttons: Always combine, hide labels
  Keeps the taskbar tidy when many windows are open.

[TIP] For beginners, "Lock the taskbar" is a good first step. It prevents accidental changes.

Common problems and quick fixes (desktop, Start menu, taskbar)

Problem: Icons disappeared from the desktop
Quick fixes:

- Right-click desktop, click View, ensure "Show desktop icons" is ticked.
- If the icons are there but hidden, choose larger icon view.

Problem: Start menu search feels slow
Quick fixes:

- Restart the computer.
- Reduce startup clutter later (we cover this in maintenance chapters).
- Keep fewer heavy programs running at once.

Problem: Taskbar moved to the side
Quick fixes:

- Right-click taskbar, untick "Lock the taskbar" if locked.
- Drag the taskbar back to the bottom.

- Right-click taskbar, tick "Lock the taskbar" again.

Problem: Too many windows open and you feel lost
Quick fixes:

- Use Alt + Tab to see what is open.//
- Close windows you do not need.
- Use the taskbar to switch instead of opening the same program again.

[TRY IT NOW] Practice tasks for this chapter

Do these on your computer right now. This is how the skills become real.

1. Desktop cleanup practice

- Create a folder on the desktop named Practice.
- Put one test file inside it (a text file or any small file).
- Delete the test file, then restore it from Recycle Bin.

2. Start menu search practice

- Press the Windows key.

- Type: calculator
- Press Enter.
- Close Calculator.
- Press Windows key again.
- Type: control panel
- Press Enter.

3. Taskbar pinning practice

- Open your browser.
- Right-click its taskbar icon.
- Pin it to the taskbar.
- Close the browser.
- Press Windows key + 1 (or click the pinned icon) to reopen it.

4. Switching practice

- Open two programs (example: Notepad and Calculator).
- Use Alt + Tab to switch between them five times.

- Use the taskbar to switch between them five times.

When you can do these without thinking, Windows 7 starts to feel easy.

CHAPTER SIX: WORKING WITH FILES AND FOLDERS THE RIGHT WAY

If Windows 7 feels confusing, it is often because of one thing: files and folders feel like they "disappear." You download something, save something, move something, and later you cannot find it. Or you edit a document and end up with two copies and you do not know which one is the latest.

This chapter fixes that.

By the end, you will be able to do these four things confidently:

- open Windows Explorer and understand what you are looking at

- create folders with clear names that make sense months later

- copy, move, delete, and restore files without fear

- find files fast using search, even when you forgot where you saved them

Windows Explorer basics

Windows Explorer is the file manager in Windows 7. It is the tool you use to browse your computer's storage, open folders, and manage files.

You can open it in several ways:

[STEP] Open Windows Explorer (easy methods)
Method A

1. Click Start.

2. Click Computer.

Method B

1. Press Windows key + E.

Method C

1. Click the folder icon on the taskbar (if it is pinned).

When Windows Explorer opens, you will see a window with a lot of parts. Do not let it intimidate you. Most of the time, you only need to understand five areas.

1) The title bar

This shows the name of the folder you are currently viewing.

2) The address bar (very important)

This shows where you are. It is like a road sign. It might look like:

Computer > Local Disk (C:) > Users > John > Documents

That line is your location. If you understand the address bar, you will almost never feel lost.

[TIP] Click inside the address bar
When you click the address bar, Windows can show the full path as text. This is useful when you want to copy a location or confirm exactly where you are.

3) The navigation pane (left side)

This shows shortcuts to common places like:

- Favorites
- Libraries
- Computer
- Network

You can use it like a map. Click a place, and the right side shows what is inside.

4) The main file list (right side)

This is the real content of the folder. It shows files and folders.

5) The search box (top-right)

This is how you search inside a folder. It is one of the fastest tools in Windows 7.

Understanding common locations in Windows 7

Beginners often store files in random places. Later they cannot remember where they saved them. The easiest fix is to learn the standard places Windows expects you to use.

Libraries

Libraries are not exactly folders. They are collections that show files from one or more locations.

Common libraries include:

- Documents

- Pictures

- Music

- Videos

If you save your work inside Documents, you can find it easily later.

[TIP] Use Documents as your default home
For most people, "Documents" should be the main place for Word files, PDFs, and anything related to writing and office work.

Computer

This shows your drives, such as:

- Local Disk (C:)
- Local Disk (D:) if you have a second partition
- USB drives
- External hard drives
- DVD drive

[NOTE] C: is usually the system drive
Most programs install on C:. Your personal files can also be stored there, but they should be organized inside your user folder.

The user folder

A common path looks like:

C:\Users\YourName\Documents

This is where your personal work should live, not inside random system folders.

Folder views that make your life easier

Windows Explorer can show your files in different views.

[STEP] Change the view

1. Open a folder.

2. Click the View button (often near the top).

3. Choose a view like:

    o Details (best for work)

    o List

    o Medium icons (good for pictures)

Why "Details" view is powerful
In Details view, you can see:

- Name

- Date modified

- Type

- Size

For real work, Date modified helps you find the latest version quickly.

[TIP] Sort by Date modified

1. Click the "Date modified" column header.

2. The newest files will rise to the top (or bottom, depending on direction).
   This instantly solves the "which one is latest?" problem.

Creating folders and naming rules

Folders are how you stay organized. A folder is like a physical file cabinet. If you name folders well, you will not need to rely on memory later.

The beginner mistake

Many people name folders like:

- New Folder

- My Stuff

- Documents 1

- Work

- Important

These names are too broad. They make sense today, but they will confuse you later.

The goal of a good folder name

A good folder name answers at least one of these:

- What is it about?

- Who is it for?

- When is it from?

Simple folder naming rules that work

Rule 1: Be specific

Bad: Work
Better: Work Reports
Best: YoCare Reports 2026

Rule 2: Keep names short but clear

You do not need a full sentence. You need a label.

Good examples:

- Photos Nairobi 2016

- Contracts 2025

- Receipts January 2026

- CV and Certificates

Rule 3: Use dates in a consistent format

For folders that grow over time, dates help a lot.

Recommended format:

- 2026-02 (Year-Month)
- 2026-02-04 (Year-Month-Day)

This format sorts in correct order automatically.

Examples:

- 2026-02 Projects
- 2026-02-04 Meeting Notes

Rule 4: Avoid special characters that Windows does not allow

Windows folder names cannot use these characters:

\ / : * ? " < > |

If you try, Windows will refuse.

Rule 5: Use the same pattern every time

Consistency is more important than perfection.

If you always name client folders like:
ClientName - Topic - Year

Then later you can find things easily.

Creating folders (the right way)

[STEP] Create a folder

1. Open the location where you want the folder.

2. Right-click an empty area.

3. Click New.

4. Click Folder.

5. Type the name and press Enter.

[TIP] Keyboard method
In many folders, you can press Ctrl + Shift + N to create a new folder quickly.

Copy, move, delete, restore from Recycle Bin

This is where many beginners panic. They fear that one wrong click will destroy everything. The truth is: Windows gives you safe ways to undo and restore, as long as you understand the basic actions.

Copy vs Move (know the difference)

- Copy means: keep the original, create another copy somewhere else.

- Move means: take it from here and put it there, leaving nothing behind.

Real-life example

If you copy a photo from your USB drive to your computer, the photo remains on the USB and also exists on the PC.

If you move it, it leaves the USB and appears on the PC only.

[TIP] When in doubt, copy first

Copy is safer. After you confirm the copy works, you can delete the original if you want.

Copying files and folders

Method A: Copy and paste (most reliable)

[STEP] Copy and paste

1. Click the file or folder once to select it.

2. Press Ctrl + C (Copy).

3. Go to the destination folder.

4. Press Ctrl + V (Paste).

Method B: Right-click menu

[STEP] Copy via right-click

1. Right-click the file or folder.

2. Click Copy.

3. Go to destination folder.

4. Right-click empty area.

5. Click Paste.

Method C: Drag and drop (use carefully)

Dragging is fast, but it can copy or move depending on where you drag.

General behavior:

- Drag within the same drive often moves.

- Drag to a different drive often copies.

[WARNING] Dragging can surprise beginners
If you drag and later your file "vanished," you probably moved it. If you are not confident yet, use Ctrl + C and Ctrl + V instead.

[TIP] Force copy while dragging
Hold Ctrl while dragging to force a copy.

Moving files and folders

Moving is similar to copying, but you use Cut instead of Copy.

[STEP] Move using Cut and Paste

1. Select the file or folder.

2. Press Ctrl + X (Cut).

3. Go to destination folder.

4. Press Ctrl + V (Paste).

[NOTE] The item does not truly move until you paste it
Cut marks it for moving. Paste completes the move.

[TIP] If you cut something and then panic
If you cut but have not pasted yet, you can press Esc, or you can copy something else. The "cut" effect will cancel.

Renaming files and folders (so you know what is what)

Renaming is one of the best habits for staying organized.

[STEP] Rename a file or folder

1. Click it once.

2. Press F2.

3. Type the new name.

4. Press Enter.

[WARNING] Be careful with file extensions

If Windows shows extensions like .doc or .jpg, do not delete the extension unless you know what you are doing. Changing it can make the file stop opening correctly.

Deleting files and folders safely

There are two kinds of delete:

- Normal delete (goes to Recycle Bin)
- Permanent delete (skips Recycle Bin)

Normal delete

[STEP] Normal delete

1. Select the item.

2. Press Delete.

3. Confirm if asked.

It goes to the Recycle Bin, so you can restore it later.

Permanent delete

[WARNING] Permanent delete is dangerous
Shift + Delete removes the item permanently. It often cannot be restored easily.

Use Shift + Delete only when:

- you are completely sure
- you have a backup
- you do not need recovery options

Restoring from Recycle Bin

If you deleted something by mistake, the Recycle Bin is your first rescue tool.

[STEP] Restore a deleted file

1. Double-click Recycle Bin on the desktop.
2. Find the item.
3. Right-click it.
4. Click Restore.

Windows sends it back to where it was before deletion.

[TIP] Sort Recycle Bin by Date Deleted
This helps when you deleted something recently and want to find it fast.

[WARNING] Emptying the Recycle Bin removes your safety net
Before emptying, scan quickly. If unsure, leave it for a while.

Finding files fast using search

Search is the skill that saves time when your memory fails.

There are two main searches you should use:

- Start menu search (general search)
- Windows Explorer search (search inside folders)

Start menu search (good for quick finds)

[STEP] Use Start menu search for a file

1. Press Windows key.
2. Type part of the file name.
3. Look under Documents or Files.
4. Click the result.

This works best when:

- the file is in Documents, Pictures, or Libraries

- you remember part of the name

Windows Explorer search (best for serious searching)

Windows Explorer has a search box at the top-right of every folder window.

Key idea: Explorer search searches within the folder you are currently viewing.

So if you search inside Documents, it searches Documents.

If you search inside Computer, it tries to search across drives, which can be slower.

[STEP] Search inside Documents

1. Open Documents.

2. Click in the search box.

3. Type part of the name.

4. Wait for results.

[TIP] Start broad, then narrow
If you only remember "report," search "report" first. Then add more words like "report 2026" or "report feb".

Searching when you do not remember the exact file name

If you forgot the name, search by clues:

Clue 1: File type

If you know it was a Word document, search inside Documents and look at the "Type" column in Details view.

You can also sort by Type.

Clue 2: Date modified

If you worked on it recently:

1. Open Documents.

2. Switch to Details view.

3. Sort by Date modified.

4. Look near the top for recent work.

This is often faster than search.

Clue 3: Search for a phrase inside the document

Some documents can be found by searching a word you remember from inside the file. This depends on indexing and file type, but it can work.

Example:
If you remember the document contained the word "budget," try searching "budget" in Documents.

Common search problems and quick fixes

Problem: Search is slow
Fixes:

- Search inside a specific folder, not across the whole computer.

- Use fewer words first, then narrow.

Problem: Search shows too many results
Fixes:

- Add another keyword.

- Sort results by Date modified.

- Check the folder path in the address bar so you know where each result is located.

Problem: Search does not find what you know exists
Fixes:

- Confirm you are searching in the right folder.
- Check spelling.
- Try searching for part of the name only.
- Use Date modified sorting and look manually in the most likely folder.

[TRY IT NOW] Practice tasks for this chapter

Do these tasks on your computer. This is where the skill becomes real.

Practice 1: Create a clean folder structure

1. Open Documents.
2. Create a folder named: Practice Files
3. Inside it, create three folders:
   - 2026-02 Notes
   - Photos Test
   - Letters

Practice 2: Copy and move safely

1. Create a text file in Practice Files (you can right-click > New > Text Document).

2. Name it: test-note.txt

3. Copy it into 2026-02 Notes using Ctrl + C and Ctrl + V.

4. Move it into Letters using Ctrl + X and Ctrl + V.

Practice 3: Delete and restore

1. Delete test-note.txt from Letters using Delete.

2. Open Recycle Bin.

3. Restore the file.

4. Confirm it returned to Letters.

Practice 4: Find it fast

1. Open Documents.

2. Use the search box to search: test-note

3. Open the file from the search results.

If you can do these four practices without confusion, you can handle daily file work confidently.

CHAPTER SEVEN: BUILT-IN HELPERS THAT SAVE TIME

Most people use only a small slice of Windows 7. They open a browser, type documents, and copy files. But Windows 7 includes small built-in tools that quietly save time every day, especially for work, school, and office tasks.

This chapter focuses on three practical areas:

- Screenshots and simple tools you can use without installing anything

- Printing basics, including the "print to PDF" idea and when it helps in real work

- Setting default programs so files open the right way every time

These are not "advanced" skills. They are daily shortcuts that reduce frustration.

1) Screenshots and simple tools (what to use and when)

A screenshot is a picture of what is on your screen. Screenshots help when you need to:

- show someone an error message

- report a problem to a technician

- explain steps to a colleague

- capture proof of an online transaction or message

- save information quickly when copying text is not possible

Windows 7 gives you several simple options. Each has a best use.

A) Print Screen key (PrtScn): quickest basic screenshot

On most keyboards, you will see a key labeled:

- PrtScn

- PrtSc

- Print Screen

When you press Print Screen, Windows captures the screen and stores it in the clipboard. Clipboard means it is copied into temporary memory, waiting for you to paste it somewhere.

What it captures:

- the whole screen

What it does not do automatically:

- it does not save a file by itself

To save it, you must paste into a program like Paint.

[STEP] Take a full-screen screenshot and save it

1. Open the screen you want to capture.
2. Press PrtScn once.
3. Click Start.
4. Type: paint
5. Press Enter.
6. In Paint, press Ctrl + V to paste.
7. Click File > Save As.
8. Choose PNG or JPG.
9. Name the file clearly, for example: error-message-2026-02-04.png
10. Choose where to save it (Documents is a good place).
11. Click Save.

When to use this

- When you need to capture everything on the screen, including the taskbar and time.

Common beginner problem
"I pressed Print Screen, but nothing happened." That is normal. It went to the clipboard. You must paste it.

B) Alt + Print Screen: screenshot of the active window only

Sometimes your desktop is messy, and you only want the error window, not everything.

Alt + PrtScn captures only the window you are currently using.

[STEP] Capture only the current window

1. Click the window you want to capture (example: an error message box).

2. Hold Alt and press PrtScn.

3. Open Paint.

4. Press Ctrl + V.

5. Save the image.

When to use this

- When you want a clean screenshot of one program window without background clutter.

C) Snipping Tool: best tool for clean screenshots

Windows 7 includes Snipping Tool. This is the best screenshot tool for beginners because it lets you select exactly what you want.

What it can do:

- capture a rectangle area
- capture a free-form shape
- capture a window
- capture the full screen
- save directly without using Paint

[STEP] Open Snipping Tool

1. Click Start.
2. Type: snipping tool
3. Press Enter.

[STEP] Take a rectangle snip

1. In Snipping Tool, click New.
2. Drag your mouse to select the area you want.
3. Release the mouse.
4. Click the Save icon.
5. Choose a name and location.
6. Save as PNG for best clarity.

When to use this

- When you only need part of the screen, like an error message, a web page section, or a specific setting.

[TIP] Use Snipping Tool for technical support
If you are asking someone for help, a Snipping Tool screenshot is often better than a long explanation.

D) Sticky Notes: quick reminders without opening Word

Sticky Notes is a simple built-in app that lets you write short notes on the desktop.

When it helps

- writing quick tasks you do not want to forget

- jotting passwords temporarily (be careful with privacy)
- keeping a short checklist visible while working

[STEP] Open Sticky Notes

1. Click Start.
2. Type: sticky notes
3. Press Enter.

[WARNING] Privacy note
Do not store sensitive passwords or private information in Sticky Notes if other people use the computer.

E) Calculator: more powerful than most beginners expect

Windows 7 Calculator has modes:

- Standard
- Scientific
- Programmer
- Statistics

When it helps

- quick math during budgeting
- conversions and percentages
- simple calculations while writing reports

[STEP] Switch calculator mode

1. Open Calculator.
2. Click View.
3. Choose the mode you want.

F) Notepad and WordPad: simple writing tools

Notepad:

- best for plain text
- useful for quick notes, copying code, or removing formatting

WordPad:

- supports basic formatting
- useful when Word is not installed

When Notepad is useful

- when you want text with no formatting

- when you copy text from the internet and want it clean

[TIP] If text looks messy when pasted into Word

Paste it into Notepad first, then copy from Notepad into Word. This removes weird formatting.

2) Printing basics and the "print to PDF" idea

Printing can feel confusing because there are two things involved:

- the document you want to print
- the printer and its settings

If either side is wrong, printing fails.

Let's make printing simple.

A) The basic printing workflow

[STEP] Print a document (basic)

1. Open the file (Word document, PDF, etc.).
2. Press Ctrl + P (this opens the print window in many programs).
3. Choose the correct printer.

4. Choose page range:

    o All pages

    o Current page

    o Pages (type numbers like 1-3,5)

5. Choose number of copies.

6. Click Print.

Common beginner mistake
Printing to the wrong printer. This happens in offices where multiple printers exist.

Always check the printer name.

B) Print preview: the best habit before wasting paper

Many programs have Print Preview. Use it if available.

Print preview shows:

- page layout
- margins
- how many pages you will print
- whether something is cut off

When to use it

- before printing long documents
- before printing forms
- when printing from a web page

C) Understanding printer statuses and basic fixes

If printing fails, check the printer status first.

[STEP] Check printer status

1. Click Start.
2. Click Devices and Printers.
3. Find your printer.

You may see statuses like:

- Ready (good)
- Offline (not connected)
- Paused (jobs are stopped)
- Error (something is wrong)

Quick fixes

- If Offline: check cables or Wi-Fi connection, then restart the printer.

- If Paused: right-click printer, click "See what's printing," then unpause.

- If jobs are stuck: cancel print jobs and restart printer.

[TIP] Restarting solves many printing issues
Restart the printer first. If needed, restart the computer second.

D) "Print to PDF" idea: what it means and why it helps

Printing to PDF means creating a PDF file instead of printing on paper.

It is useful when you need to:

- submit a document online

- share a final version that looks the same on any computer

- protect formatting

- keep a record of an invoice, report, or form

Windows 7 does not always include a built-in "Print to PDF" printer by default. But the idea still matters because many workplaces use PDF printers, and many programs can export to PDF.

So think of it as:
"Print, but the output is a PDF file."

How it fits in real work

- You fill a form, print to PDF, and email it.

- You create a report, print to PDF, and upload it to a portal.

- You convert a webpage receipt into a PDF for recordkeeping.

[TIP] If you do not see a PDF printer
Look for export options in the program like:

- Save As PDF

- Export PDF

If you do have a PDF printer installed, it will show in the printer list like any other printer. When you click Print, it will ask where to save the PDF file.

3) Setting default programs for common file types

A default program is the app Windows uses automatically to open a file type.

Example:

- Double-click a .jpg photo. It opens in the default photo viewer.

- Double-click a .pdf file. It opens in the default PDF reader.

When defaults are wrong, you get problems like:

- photos opening in the wrong program

- PDF files opening in a browser when you prefer a PDF reader

- documents opening in WordPad instead of Word

The solution is to set defaults properly once, then enjoy smooth opening forever.

A) Set default programs using "Open with"

This is the simplest method when only one file type is wrong.

[STEP] Change default program using Open with

1. Right-click the file (example: a PDF).

2. Click Open with.

3. Click Choose default program…

4. Select the program you want.

5. Tick the box:
   "Always use the selected program to open this kind of file."

6. Click OK.

Now all files of that type will open with that program.

B) Set default programs through Control Panel

This method is more complete and gives you a list of defaults.

[STEP] Set defaults through Control Panel

1. Click Start.

2. Click Control Panel.

3. Click Programs.

4. Click Default Programs.

5. Choose one:

   o   Set your default programs

- Associate a file type or protocol with a program

If you want to set many file types for one program, use "Set your default programs."

If you want to fix one file type, use "Associate a file type…"

C) Recommended defaults for common file types

These are practical common choices:

- .pdf: a dedicated PDF reader (not a random browser plugin)

- .jpg, .png: Windows Photo Viewer or a trusted image tool

- .doc, .docx: Microsoft Word (if installed)

- .xls, .xlsx: Microsoft Excel (if installed)

- .txt: Notepad (simple and safe)

- audio/video: Windows Media Player or another trusted media player

[NOTE] Choose defaults based on your daily work
If you always edit photos in a specific program, set that as default.

[TRY IT NOW] Practice tasks

1. Screenshot practice

- Open any window (Control Panel is fine).

- Use Snipping Tool to capture a small area.

- Save it to Documents with a clear name.

2. Printing practice (even if you do not have a printer)

- Open a document.

- Press Ctrl + P to see the print window.

- Observe the printer list and page options.

- Cancel the print (do not print).

3. Default program practice

- Right-click a photo or PDF.

- Use Open with to set a default (only if you actually want to change it).

- Confirm by double-clicking another file of the same type.

BACK MATTER

You have reached the end of the main learning journey. If you read and practiced even half of what this book covered, you are no longer a beginner in the old sense of the word. You now know how to install or upgrade Windows 7, use the desktop and files confidently, manage devices and programs, adjust settings, keep the system maintained, and troubleshoot the problems that most people panic over.

This back matter is built to serve as a "quick reference" section. You can return here when you forget a shortcut, when you want a weekly routine, or when you see a Windows word you do not understand.

Quick Keyboard Shortcuts Sheet

These shortcuts save time. You do not need to memorize them all at once. Start with the ones you will use daily, then add more.

Everyday navigation and window control

- Windows key: Open Start menu

- Windows key + D: Show desktop (toggle)

- Windows key + E: Open Windows Explorer

- Windows key + L: Lock the computer
- Windows key + R: Open Run dialog
- Windows key + U: Open Ease of Access Center
- Windows key + P: Projector options (Duplicate, Extend, etc.)
- Windows key + Pause/Break: System information window

Switching and closing

- Alt + Tab: Switch between open programs
- Alt + F4: Close the current window or program
- Ctrl + Shift + Esc: Open Task Manager
- Ctrl + Alt + Delete: Security screen (lock, Task Manager option, etc.)

Copy, paste, and file work

- Ctrl + C: Copy
- Ctrl + X: Cut
- Ctrl + V: Paste

- Ctrl + Z: Undo

- Ctrl + A: Select all

- Delete: Send item to Recycle Bin

- Shift + Delete: Permanently delete (use carefully)

- F2: Rename selected file/folder

Browser and text editing basics

- Ctrl + F: Find on page or in some documents

- Ctrl + S: Save

- Ctrl + P: Print

- Ctrl + T: New browser tab

- Ctrl + W: Close current tab

- Ctrl + Shift + T: Reopen closed tab (in many browsers)

- Ctrl + Plus (+): Zoom in (in many browsers)

- Ctrl + Minus (-): Zoom out (in many browsers)

- Ctrl + 0: Reset zoom (in many browsers)

Screenshots and screen tools

- PrtScn (Print Screen): Copy entire screen to clipboard

- Alt + PrtScn: Copy active window to clipboard

- Windows key + P: (Also useful for display setup, especially with projectors)

Note: Windows 7 does not include the modern Snipping Tool shortcut, but Snipping Tool exists and can be opened from Start menu search: "snipping tool".

Windows 7 Maintenance Schedule (Weekly, Monthly)

Maintenance is what keeps a Windows 7 PC stable over time. This schedule is designed for real life. It focuses on actions that make the biggest difference without turning you into a technician.

Weekly maintenance (15 to 30 minutes)

1. Restart the PC at least once

- Many small issues disappear after a restart.

- Restart also helps Windows complete pending tasks.

2. Check disk free space quickly

- Computer → right-click C: → Properties

- If free space is getting low, plan cleanup soon.

3. Run a quick antivirus scan (if installed)

- Quick scan catches common threats early.

4. Look at Action Center warnings

- Control Panel → System and Security → Action Center

- Fix red warnings first.

5. Clean your Downloads folder lightly

- Remove duplicate installers and files you no longer need.

Optional weekly:

- Run Disk Cleanup if you browse heavily or download a lot.

Monthly maintenance (45 to 90 minutes)

1. Windows Update check

- Open Windows Update

- Install important updates

- Restart afterward if required

2. Disk Cleanup (deep)

- Run Disk Cleanup

- Use "Clean up system files" if you need more space

- Be careful with service pack backups and anything that reduces rollback options

3. Review installed programs

- Control Panel → Programs and Features

- Uninstall anything you do not use or do not recognize (after careful checking)

4. Startup program review (if boot is getting slow)

- msconfig → Startup tab

- Disable only what you recognize and do not need at startup

5. Defragment (HDD only)

- Disk Defragmenter
- Analyze first
- Defragment if needed
- Skip this if you have an SSD

6. Back up important files

- Copy documents, photos, and critical work to external drive or trusted storage
- Backups matter more than optimization

Every 3 to 6 months (deeper health check)

1. Check your browser add-ons and toolbars

- Remove anything you do not use or trust.

2. Review drivers only if something is not working

- Device Manager
- Do not update drivers "for fun"
- Update drivers when you have a reason

3. Consider disk error checking

- Right-click C: → Properties → Tools → Error-checking

- Run when the PC is stable and you can restart if needed

Glossary of Common Windows Words

This glossary explains words you will see in Windows 7 and in help articles. Read it like a dictionary. It is here so you do not get stuck on vocabulary.

Administrator

A user account with full control over the computer. Administrators can install software and change system settings.

Adapter (Network adapter)

The hardware that connects your computer to a network, such as Wi-Fi or Ethernet.

Backup

A copy of your important files stored somewhere else, so you can recover them if the computer fails.

Control Panel

The main Windows area where you change system settings.

Driver

Software that allows Windows to communicate with hardware, such as printers, Wi-Fi, sound, and graphics.

Disk Cleanup

A Windows tool that removes temporary and unnecessary files to free storage space.

Disk Defragmenter

A Windows tool that rearranges fragmented files on a traditional hard drive (HDD) to improve performance.

Firewall

A security tool that helps block unwanted network traffic.

Folder

A container used to organize files.

Fragmentation

When a file is split into pieces on a traditional hard drive, causing slower reads.

Hard drive (HDD)

Traditional storage device with moving parts. Slower than SSD. Benefits from defragmentation.

SSD (Solid State Drive)

Modern storage device with no moving parts. Fast. Does not need defragmentation.

HomeGroup

A Windows feature that makes sharing files and printers easier on a home network.

Internet Protocol (IP)

A system that gives devices addresses on a network. If IP addressing fails, internet may show limited access.

Malware

Harmful software such as viruses, spyware, and unwanted programs.

msconfig (System Configuration)

A tool used to control startup programs and services.

Network discovery

A Windows setting that allows your computer to see other computers and devices on the network.

Operating system (OS)

The main software that runs the computer and manages hardware and programs. Windows 7 is an operating system.

Process

A running program or background task shown in Task Manager.

Program (Application)

Software you install and use, such as a browser, office tools, or media players.

Restore point

A saved system state used by System Restore to roll back changes.

System Restore

A Windows feature that rolls back system settings to an earlier point without deleting personal files.

Task Manager

A tool that shows running programs, processes, and performance usage.

Update

A software patch or improvement. Updates can fix security, stability, and compatibility issues.

Windows Explorer

The file manager used to browse files and folders in Windows.

INDEX

This index is written for beginners, so you can find topics quickly. Items are grouped by main words you will remember.

A

- Action Center
- Administrator account
- Add a printer
- Add a device
- Advanced SystemCare (optional)
- Adapter settings

B

- Backup basics
- Boot options (USB/DVD)
- Browsers (toolbars, add-ons)
- Built-in troubleshooters

C

- ClearType text

- Clock settings
- Control Panel map
- Copy, move, delete files

D

- Date and time
- Defragmenter (HDD)
- Device Manager
- Devices and Printers
- Disk Cleanup
- Drivers

E

- Ease of Access Center
- Error checking (disk)
- Editions of Windows 7
- Extend vs Duplicate (projector)

F

- File sharing

- Files and folders
- Firewall basics
- Freeing space

G

- Graphics driver
- Glossary

H

- Hardware and Sound
- HomeGroup
- High contrast themes

I

- Installing Windows 7
- Internet Time sync
- IP address and limited access

K

- Keyboard layouts
- Keyboard shortcuts sheet

L

- Language and region
- Limited access (network)

M

- Magnifier
- Maintenance schedule
- Malware symptoms
- msconfig

N

- Network and Sharing Center
- Network discovery
- Network troubleshooting

P

- Parental controls
- Performance Information and Tools
- Printer problems
- Programs and Features

R

- Recovery tools (Safe Mode, Startup Repair)
- Region and Language
- Recycle Bin
- Restore points

S

- Safe Mode
- Scheduling defrag
- Screen resolution
- Services and Windows Update
- Speech recognition
- Startup programs
- System Restore
- System and Maintenance

T

- Task Manager
- Troubleshooters

- Toolbars (browser)

U

- Uninstalling safely
- Updates (Windows Update)

W

- Windows Features on/off
- Windows Explorer
- Windows Update routine
- Wireless connections

FINAL NOTE TO THE READER

If you finished this book, you did something most people never do. You chose to understand your computer instead of fearing it.

Windows 7 can feel intimidating at first, not because it is impossible, but because it has many doors. Control Panel, updates, drivers, networks, permissions, backups. When you do not know which door to open, every problem feels like a disaster. Now you do know. And that changes everything.

Here is the simple truth that keeps a PC healthy for years.

Keep space on the C: drive.
Install updates when you can.
Remove programs you do not use.
Back up what you cannot afford to lose.
Fix problems using a calm checklist, not random clicks.

You do not need to become a technician. You only need a few good habits.

Also remember this: performance is not only about speed. It is about reliability. A computer that starts quickly but loses your files is not a good computer. A computer that looks clean but has no backups is not safe. A computer that has many "boost" tools but still crashes is not improved.

So keep it simple. Use Windows tools first. Use optional tools only when you understand what they change. And whenever you make a big change, create a restore point and make a backup.

If you want to go further, the next level is practice. Help a friend set up a user account. Fix a printer issue using Device Manager. Clean a crowded drive properly. Set up two clocks for two cities. These small wins build real confidence.

Thank you for reading, and for taking your computer skills seriously. You are not just using a PC anymore. You are managing it.

ABOUT THE AUTHOR

John Monyjok Maluth is a practical technology guide writer and an ICT and Communication Officer with hands-on experience supporting real users in real work environments.

He has worked on everyday Windows tasks that matter to beginners and office teams, including installing and maintaining systems, setting up user accounts, managing essential applications, supporting connectivity and printing, and keeping computers stable through disciplined maintenance habits.

He also writes and teaches with a simple goal: make skills clear, usable, and honest. His personal vision is Inspiration, his mission is Empowerment, and his guiding value is Integrity. That shows up in the way he explains technology: no hype, no fear, just steps that work.

www.ingramcontent.com/pod-product-compliance
Lightning Source LLC
Chambersburg PA
CBHW020657220526
45464CB00001B/480